Turning Green Thumbs into Greenbacks: How to Start a Thriving Landscaping Business

By Silas Meadowlark

Index

- Laying the Foundation
    - Assessing Your Passion for Landscaping
    - Identifying Your Unique Skills and Strengths
    - Conducting Market Research

- Developing a Winning Business Plan
    - Crafting a Comprehensive Vision and Mission
    - Defining Your Target Market and Services
    - Projecting Financial Forecasts and Budgets

- Choosing the Right Legal Structure
    - Sole Proprietorship, Partnership, or Corporation?
    - Registering Your Business and Obtaining Licenses
    - Understanding Tax Implications and Obligations

- Building a Powerful Brand Identity
    - Designing a Memorable Logo and Branding
    - Establishing a Professional Online Presence
    - Creating Marketing Materials that Shine

- Acquiring the Necessary Equipment
    - Investing in Essential Landscaping Tools
    - Maintaining and Upgrading Your Equipment
    - Ensuring Proper Storage and Maintenance

- Assembling a Skilled Team
    - Recruiting and Hiring Talented Employees
    - Providing Comprehensive Training Programs
    - Fostering a Positive and Productive Culture

- Mastering the Art of Pricing
    - Calculating Accurate Cost Estimates
    - Determining Competitive Pricing Strategies

- Offering Flexible Payment Options

- Streamlining Operations and Workflows
  - Developing Efficient Scheduling and Routing
  - Implementing Effective Inventory Management
  - Utilizing Technology to Boost Productivity

- Winning and Retaining Customers
  - Leveraging Networking and Referrals
  - Delivering Exceptional Customer Service
  - Building Long-Term Relationships

- Expanding Your Service Offerings
  - Exploring Complementary Landscaping Services
  - Diversifying Your Product and Service Mix
  - Adapting to Changing Market Demands

- Navigating Regulatory Compliance
  - Understanding Local Zoning and Permit Laws
  - Complying with Environmental Regulations
  - Ensuring Worker Safety and Liability Coverage

- Mastering Effective Marketing Strategies
  - Developing a Comprehensive Marketing Plan
  - Utilizing Traditional and Digital Advertising
  - Leveraging Social Media and Online Platforms

- Scaling Your Business for Growth
  - Identifying Opportunities for Expansion
  - Streamlining Processes and Automating Tasks
  - Securing Financing and Investing in Infrastructure

- Managing Finances and Cash Flow
  - Implementing Robust Accounting Practices
  - Monitoring Income, Expenses, and Profitability
  - Exploring Financing Options and Tax Incentives

- Ensuring Long-Term Sustainability
  - Fostering Environmentally-Friendly Practices

- Investing in Employee Development and Retention
- Continuously Innovating and Adapting to the Market

Laying the Foundation

Assessing Your Passion for Landscaping

So, you've got a green thumb and a penchant for transforming outdoor spaces into verdant oases? Excellent! But before you jump headfirst into the landscaping business, it's time to take a step back and really examine your passion for the craft. After all, this isn't just a passing fancy – it's a lifelong commitment to the art of shaping the great outdoors.

Start by asking yourself some probing questions: What is it about landscaping that sets your soul on fire? Is it the thrill of sketching out complicated garden designs, the satisfaction of watching a carefully curated collection of plants burst into bloom, or the joy of creating peaceful sanctuaries for your clients? Dig deep and uncover the roots of your fascination with the natural world.

Next, consider your level of dedication. Are you the type who can spend hours meticulously pruning hedges, or do you prefer the fast paced adrenaline rush of executing grand setting transformations? Understand your strengths and limitations, as they'll play a vital role in shaping the direction of your budding business.

Remember, building a thriving landscaping venture requires more than just a green thumb – it's a labor of love that demands your unwavering commitment. So, take the time to truly reflect on your passion and ensure that it runs as deep as the roots of your favorite oak tree. Only then can you confidently initiate on your journey to turn those green thumbs into greenbacks.

Identifying Your Unique Skills and Strengths

Now that you've reconnected with your passion for landscaping, it's time to take a closer look at the skills and strengths you bring to the table. After all, the key to standing out in a crowded market is to capitalize on what makes you truly unique.

Start by conducting a thorough self assessment. What are your areas of expertise? Are you a master at crafting breathtaking garden designs, or do you excel at the meticulous task of plant cultivation? Perhaps you have a knack for understanding the complex needs of different soil types or a keen eye for identifying the perfect placement of hardscaping elements.

Don't just focus on your technical abilities, either. Consider your soft skills – your ability to communicate effectively with clients, your tireless work ethic, or your talent for problem solving on the fly. These qualities can often be the difference between a good landscaper and a great one.

Once you've identified your strengths, it's time to let them shine. Develop a clear understanding of how your unique skills can benefit your clients and set you apart from the competition. Weave these strengths into your marketing materials, underline them during client consultations, and let them guide the way you approach every landscaping project.

Remember, your strengths are the foundation upon which you'll build your thriving landscaping business. Embrace them, nurture them, and let them blossom like the carefully tended gardens you'll create for your clients.

Conducting Market Research

Now that you've taken the time to reflect on your passion and identify your unique strengths, it's time to turn your gaze outward and explore the ever evolving terrain of the landscaping industry.

Begin by examining your local market. What are the current trends and demands in your area? Are homeowners gravitating towards low maintenance, drought resistant landscaping, or are they clamoring for meticulously manicured, traditional gardens? Identify the is a problem and desires of your potential clients, and use this knowledge to shape your service options.

Next, dive into the competition. Scope out the other landscaping businesses in your region, and analyze their strengths, weaknesses, and unique selling propositions. How do they market themselves? What services do they provide? By understanding your competitors, you'll be better equipped to carve out your own niche and offer something that truly sets you apart.

Don't forget to keep an eye on the broader industry as well. Stay up to-date on the latest landscaping technologies, design trends, and environmental regulations. This knowledge will not only help you provide the most cutting edge services to your clients but also position you as an industry authority.

Finally, don't be afraid to get your hands dirty – literally. Spend time in the field, observing the work of other landscapers, chatting with potential clients, and immersing yourself in the unique challenges and opportunities of your local market. This firsthand experience will be indispensable as you fine tune your business strategy and position yourself for success.

Remember, thorough market research is the foundation upon which you'll build a thriving landscaping business. So, dive in, embrace your inner data cruncher, and let the perceptions you uncover guide you towards a future filled with lush gardens and satisfied clients.

Developing a Winning Business Plan

Crafting a Comprehensive Vision and Mission

Alright, folks, buckle up because we're about to dive headfirst into the heart of your landscaping empire - your business plan. Now, I know what you're thinking: "Business plan? That's about as exciting as watching grass grow." But trust me, this is where the magic happens, the place where you'll lay the foundation for your journey to financial freedom.

Let's start with the big picture, shall we? It's time to craft a vision and mission that will act as the guiding light for your landscaping business. This isn't just some fluffy, feel good mumbo jumbo - it's the DNA that will shape every decision you make, from the types of services you offer to the way you interact with your clients.

Now, I'm not talking about some generic, cookie cutter mission statement that sounds like it was written by a committee of corporate robots. No, sir. We're going to dig deep, tap into that green thumbed passion of yours, and create something that's as unique and vibrant as the beautiful sets the scene you'll be creating.

Picture this: you're standing in front of a lush, perfectly manicured garden, the sun glistening off the freshly cut grass, and you can't help but feel a sense of pride swell within you. That's the kind of energy you want to bottle up and pour into your vision and mission. Think big, think bold, and think about the impact you want to have on your community.

Once you've got that vision and mission locked in, it's time to start painting the picture of your target market. Who are the people you want to work with? What are their is a problem, their desires, their landscaping dreams? Get to know them like they're your best friends, because the more you understand your audience, the better you'll be able to serve them.

Defining Your Target Market and Services

Now, I know what you're thinking: "But I want to work with everyone! The more clients, the more money, right?" Wrong, my friend. That's a surefire way to stretch yourself thin and end up hating every second of this business venture. No, the key is to laser focus on the clients who are the perfect fit for your services.

Start by segmenting your target market into distinct groups - maybe it's residential homeowners, commercial property managers, or even high end luxury clients. Each group will have different needs, budgets, and expectations, so you'll need to tailor your products accordingly.

Once you've identified your target market, it's time to get to work on your service options. This is where you can really let your creativity shine. Think beyond the standard mowing and edging - how about specialty garden design, tree pruning, or even seasonal flower installations? The possibilities are endless, so don't be afraid to get a little wild and original.

Remember, the key is to differentiate yourself from the competition. Maybe you're the only landscaper in town who specializes in drought resistant gardens, or perhaps you're the go to expert for creating stunning rooftop oases. Whatever your niche, make sure it coordinates with the needs and desires of your target market.

And let's not forget about pricing. This is where you'll need to put on your finance hat and start crunching some numbers. Research the going rates in your local market, factor in your costs and overhead, and then add a healthy dose of value based pricing. Remember, your clients aren't just paying for the physical work - they're paying for your expertise, your creativity, and the peace of mind that comes with working with a true professional.

Projecting Financial Forecasts and Budgets

Alright, let's talk money, honey. Because let's be honest, at the end of the day, this is a business, and if you want to turn those green thumbs into greenbacks, you're going to need to get your financial ducks in a row.

First up, let's tackle those financial forecasts. Break out your crystal ball and start envisioning the future of your landscaping empire. How many clients do you expect to have in the first year? What about the second and third? What kind of revenue will those clients bring in, and how much will it cost you to service them?

Now, I know what you're thinking: "But I don't have a crystal ball, and my future telling skills are a little rusty." No worries, my friend. This is where your good old fashioned research and data crunching skills come into play. Look at industry trends, analyze your local market, and don't be afraid to reach out to other landscaping pros for a little insider knowledge.

Once you've got those financial projections dialed in, it's time to start building your budget. This is where the real magic happens, folks. You'll need to factor in everything from equipment costs and employee salaries to marketing expenses and insurance premiums. And don't forget to leave a little wiggle room for those unexpected curveballs that always seem to pop up when you least expect them.

Remember, a well crafted budget isn't just a boring spreadsheet - it's the roadmap that will guide you to financial success. Keep it updated, monitor it religiously, and use it as a tool to make informed decisions that will keep your landscaping business growing and thriving.

Choosing the Right Legal Structure

Sole Proprietorship, Partnership, or Corporation?

When it comes to starting your landscaping business, the first important decision you'll face is choosing the right legal structure. This choice will have far reaching implications for your operations, taxes, and liability, so it's essential to weigh the pros and cons of each option with care. Let's dive in and explore the three primary structures: sole proprietorship, partnership, and corporation.

The sole proprietorship is the simplest and most straightforward option, often favored by entrepreneurs just starting out. As a sole proprietor, you'll be the sole owner of your business, with complete control over decision making and the ability to keep all the profits. However, this also means you'll bear full responsibility for any debts or liabilities incurred by the business. Your personal assets, such as your home or savings, could be at risk if things take a turn for the worse.

For those looking to share the load and the rewards, a partnership may be the way to go. Here, you'll team up with one or more individuals, combining your skills, resources, and capital. The upside? You get to split the workload and make use of each other's strengths. The downside? You also share the liability, and disputes between partners can quickly become messy and derail your progress.

Finally, there's the more formal and structured option of a

corporation. As a corporation, your business is considered a separate legal entity, shielding your personal assets from the company's obligations and liabilities. This added protection comes with more complex administrative requirements, such as maintaining corporate records, holding shareholder meetings, and submitting annual reports. However, the potential benefits of greater credibility, access to funding, and tax advantages may make it a worthwhile consideration, especially as your landscaping business grows.

Ultimately, the choice of legal structure will depend on your specific goals, risk tolerance, and long term aspirations for your landscaping enterprise. Take the time to research each option thoroughly, consult with legal and financial advisors, and select the structure that coordinates best with your vision for the future.

Registering Your Business and Obtaining Licenses

Once you've decided on the right legal structure for your landscaping business, it's time to get the necessary registrations and licenses in place. This step is important, as it ensures your operations are compliant with local, state, and federal regulations.

Depending on your chosen structure, you'll need to register your business name with the appropriate authorities. For a sole proprietorship or partnership, this may involve filing a "doing business as" (DBA) certificate. For a corporation, you'll need to officially incorporate your business with your state's secretary of state office.

Next, you'll need to obtain the necessary licenses and permits to operate your landscaping business. This could include a general business license, contractor licenses, and specific permits related to landscaping activities, such as operating heavy equipment or applying pesticides. The requirements can vary widely depending on your location, so it's essential to research the regulations in your area thoroughly.

Don't forget about tax related registrations, either. You'll need to apply for an Employer Identification Number (EIN) from the Internal Revenue Service, which will be used for filing taxes, opening a business bank account, and other financial transactions. Depending on your location, you may also need to register for state and local tax obligations, such as sales tax or payroll taxes.

Navigating the maze of paperwork and legal requirements can seem daunting, but tackle it head on. Staying compliant not only protects your business but also demonstrates your professionalism to potential clients. Consider enlisting the help of a business attorney or accountant to ensure you've covered all your bases.

Understanding Tax Implications and Obligations

Ah, taxes - the bane of every entrepreneur's existence, but a necessary evil. As a landscaping business owner, it's vital to understand the tax implications and obligations that come with your chosen legal structure.

Let's start with the sole proprietorship. As a sole proprietor, your business income and expenses will be reported on your personal tax return (Form 1040, Schedule C). This means your business profits are subject to both income tax and self employment tax, which covers Social Security and Medicare contributions. Keep meticulous records, as you'll need to track all business related income and expenses to accurately calculate your tax liability.

If you've opted for a partnership, the process becomes a bit more complex. Partnerships file their own tax return (Form 1065), but the income and deductions are "passed through" to the individual partners, who then report their share on their personal tax returns. This can get tricky when it comes to dividing profits and losses, so be sure to have a clear partnership agreement in place.

Corporations, on the other hand, are considered separate legal entities for tax purposes. As such, they pay their own federal and state corporate income taxes on the company's profits. Shareholders are then taxed on any dividends they receive from the corporation. This dual taxation can be a drawback, but the potential for tax deductions and other benefits may outweigh the costs, especially as your landscaping business grows.

Regardless of your chosen structure, be prepared to fulfill a variety of tax obligations, such as paying estimated quarterly taxes, withholding and remitting payroll taxes, and submitting annual returns. Staying on top of these requirements can be a full time job in itself, so consider enlisting the help of a qualified accountant or tax professional to ensure you're always in compliance.

Building a Powerful Brand Identity

Designing a Memorable Logo and Branding

Ah, the humble logo - a visual representation of your business that can make or break your first impression. But fear not, my landscaping friends, for crafting a captivating logo is as easy as pruning a bonsai tree. Well, maybe not quite that easy, but with the right approach, you can create a symbol that will have your clients doing a double take and wondering, "Why didn't I think of that?"

First and foremost, let's ditch the generic clipart of a lawnmower or a tree. Those are about as original as a metal garden gnome. Instead, dig deep into the essence of your business - what makes you unique, what sets you apart from the competition. Perhaps it's your unwavering commitment to eco friendly practices, or your team's unparalleled attention to detail. Whatever it is, let that be the driving force behind your logo design.

Now, I know what you're thinking: "But I'm not a graphic designer. I can barely draw a stick figure!" Fear not, my green thumbed friend, for the internet is a veritable wealth of design resources. From Canva to Fiverr, there's a world of talented creatives just waiting to bring your vision to life. Don't be afraid to get a little weird and experimental – the most memorable logos often come from the most unexpected places.

Remember, your logo is the face of your business, so treat it with the same care and attention you would a prized bonsai.

Incorporate bold colors, clean lines, and a touch of whimsy to make it truly stand out. And don't be afraid to revisit and refine your design as your business evolves. After all, a logo is a living, breathing thing, just like the greenery you so lovingly tend to.

Establishing a Professional Online Presence

In today's digital age, your online presence is the equivalent of a perfectly manicured garden – it's the first thing potential clients will see, and it can make or break their impression of your business. So, let's get to work on crafting an online oasis that will have them swooning with delight.

Start with a website that's as sleek and user friendly as a freshly mowed lawn. Ditch the clunky templates and embrace a design that reflects your brand's personality. Use high quality images of your work to showcase your landscaping prowess, and make it easy for clients to contact you with a prominent "Get a Quote" button.

But your online presence doesn't stop there, my friends. Social media is the secret weapon in your landscaping arsenal, so get ready to get your hands dirty. Platforms like Instagram and Facebook are the perfect places to showcase your work, connect with potential clients, and even offer valuable tips and advice. Just remember to keep your content fresh, engaging, and matched with your brand's unique voice.

And let's not forget about the power of online reviews. In the world of landscaping, word of-mouth is everything, so make it a priority to encourage your satisfied clients to leave glowing reviews on platforms like Google and Yelp. These testimonials can be the difference between a prospective client booking with you or your competitor down the street.

Remember, your online presence is the digital equivalent of a beautifully crafted garden – it takes time, effort, and a keen eye for detail to make it truly shine. But trust me, the rewards will be well worth it, as you watch your client base blossom and grow.

Creating Marketing Materials that Shine

Alright, let's talk about the unsung heroes of the landscaping world: your marketing materials. These little gems are the key to capturing the attention of your target audience and setting your business apart from the pack.

First up, your business cards – the humble rectangles that can make all the difference in a world of digital connections. Forget the plain, generic cards that get lost in the shuffle. Instead, embrace a design that's as unique as your landscaping skills. Maybe it's a seed packet inspired card that doubles as a mini planter, or a die cut shape that mimics the leaf of your signature tree species. The possibilities are endless, so get creative and let your brand's personality shine.

And let's not forget about your other marketing collateral – brochures, flyers, and even vehicle wraps. These are your chance to showcase your work in all its glory, so don't be afraid to pull out all the stops. Use high quality imagery, eye catching headlines, and a touch of whimsy to make your materials stand out from the crowd. Remember, you're not just selling your services – you're selling a lifestyle, a dream of lush, perfectly manicured sets the scene.

Of course, in today's digital first world, your marketing materials can't be limited to the physical realm. Embrace the power of e newsletters, social media graphics, and even video content to engage your audience and keep them coming back for more. Just remember to maintain a consistent brand voice and aesthetic across all your platforms – after all, a well tended garden doesn't just happen overnight.

So, there you have it, my landscaping friends – the keys to crafting marketing materials that will make your competitors green with envy. Now, go forth and create something so mesmerizing, your clients will be begging for a front row seat to your landscaping magic.

Acquiring the Necessary Equipment

Investing in Essential Landscaping Tools

When it comes to starting a thriving landscaping business, having the right tools for the job is vital. Think of your equipment as the foundation upon which your success will be built - without the proper gear, you'll be attempting to move mountains with a toothpick. But fear not, my green thumbed entrepreneur, for we shall navigate this essential investment with the precision of a master gardener wielding a perfectly sharpened pair of pruning shears.

First and foremost, assess your needs based on the services you plan to offer. Are you aiming to be a one stop-shop for all things lawn and garden, or do you have a more specialized niche in mind? This will inform your initial equipment purchases. From reliable lawnmowers and trimmers to heavy duty tillers and edgers, each tool should be carefully selected to maximize efficiency and deliver the high quality results your clients demand.

But equipment isn't just about the big ticket items. Don't overlook the importance of smaller, yet equally essential, tools like pruning saws, hedge clippers, rakes, and shovels. These humble implements may not grab the spotlight, but they'll be your trusty sidekicks, equipping you to tackle a wide range of landscaping tasks with precision and finesse.

And let's not forget the power tools - the ones that'll have your clients gasping in awe as you transform their overgrown yards into meticulously manicured oases. Chainsaws, stump grinders, and high powered blowers can be game changers, but approach these with caution. Ensure proper training, safety protocols, and maintenance to keep both your team and your clients out of harm's way.

Maintaining and Upgrading Your Equipment

Now that you've assembled your formidable arsenal of landscaping tools, it's time to shift your focus to maintenance and upgrades. Remember, these aren't just inanimate objects - they're the heartbeat of your business, the engines that drive your success. Treat them with the care and attention they deserve, and they'll reward you with years of reliable, high performance service.

Develop a comprehensive maintenance regimen that covers everything from regular oil changes and blade sharpening to thorough cleanings and storage procedures. Invest in a dedicated workspace or storage facility to keep your equipment protected from the elements, ensuring it's always ready to tackle the next job with the same level of power and precision as the day you first unboxed it.

But don't let your equipment stagnate - embrace the power of continuous improvement. Keep a close eye on industry trends and advancements, always staying attuned to the latest innovations that could give your business a competitive edge. Whether it's upgrading to a more fuel efficient mower or investing in a state of-the art spraying system, staying ahead of the curve will set you apart from the competition and demonstrate your commitment to providing top notch services.

Remember, your equipment is the backbone of your landscaping business, so treat it with the respect it deserves. With a meticulous maintenance routine and a willingness to evolve, you'll ensure that your tools remain as sharp, powerful, and reliable as the green thumb that wields them.

Ensuring Proper Storage and Maintenance

Ah, the unsung heroes of the landscaping world – the humble storage spaces and maintenance practices that keep your equipment in tip top shape. While they may not elicit the same level of excitement as the latest and greatest gadgets, these behind the-scenes elements are the true linchpins that will propel your business to greatness.

First and foremost, let's talk about storage. Your equipment is an investment, and it deserves to be treated with the utmost care. Invest in a dedicated storage facility, whether it's a climate controlled warehouse, a well ventilated garage, or even a meticulously organized shed. This will not only extend the lifespan of your tools but also ensure they're always ready to tackle the next job with the same level of precision and power as the day you acquired them.

But storage is just the beginning – proper maintenance is the key to uncovering the true potential of your equipment. Develop a comprehensive maintenance schedule that covers everything from regular oil changes and filter replacements to thorough cleanings and sharpening of blades. Encourage your team to take pride in the care and upkeep of your tools, instilling a sense of ownership and responsibility that will pay dividends in the long run.

And let's not forget the importance of proper storage and maintenance when it comes to hazardous materials. Fuel, lubricants, and other chemicals must be handled with the utmost care, stored in designated, well ventilated areas, and disposed of in accordance with local regulations. Neglecting these safety protocols could not only put your equipment at risk but also jeopardize the well being of your team and the environment.

So, embrace the unsung heroes of your landscaping business – the storage spaces and maintenance practices that will keep your equipment running like a well oiled machine. With a little TLC and a lot of attention to detail, your tools will become the envy of the industry, powering your way to success one manicured lawn at a time.

Assembling a Skilled Team

Recruiting and Hiring Talented Employees

Building a thriving landscaping business is no small feat, and the key to your success lies in the team you assemble. Gone are the days of relying solely on word of-mouth and hoping for the best when it comes to hiring. In this dog eat-dog world of landscaping, you need to be strategic, savvy, and downright ruthless in your pursuit of the best and brightest talent.

Start by casting a wide net – scour the depths of online job boards, reach out to your network, and don't be afraid to offer hefty referral bonuses to your current crew. Remember, the perfect candidate isn't always the one with the most manicured resume – sometimes, it's the mavericks who march to the beat of their own lawnmower.

Once you've weeded through the applicants, it's time to put on your interrogation hat. Forget the standard questions about strengths and weaknesses – dig deeper, my friend. Ask them about their dream garden design, their thoughts on the latest organic fertilizer trends, or how they'd handle a client who demands that their lawn be fashioned into the shape of a life size unicorn. The answers will separate the green thumbs from the brown ones.

And don't forget, personality is just as important as expertise. You want a team of landscaping all stars, but they also need to mesh well with your company culture. Throw in a few curveballs during the interview process – maybe a spontaneous game of lawn darts or a sudden request for them to perform a interpretive dance about the beauty of freshly mowed grass. Trust me, the results will be illuminating.

Providing Comprehensive Training Programs

Alright, so you've assembled a crack team of landscaping ninjas – now what? Time to put them through the wringer with some seriously comprehensive training programs, that's what. Remember, these aren't just your average grass cutting, shrub pruning minions – they're the lifeblood of your business, and you need to invest in their growth and development like a professional horticulturist tending to a rare, exotic bloom.

Start with the basics – safety protocols, equipment operation, and client communication. But don't stop there, oh no. Explore into the nuances of soil pH, the art of topiary sculpting, and the subtle differences between Japanese maples and Norwegian spruce. Heck, throw in a few field trips to local botanical gardens, just to really get their green juices flowing.

And don't forget the importance of cross training. Sure, you might have a team of specialized experts – the mowing maestro, the hedge trimming Hercules, the mulch maven – but the true advocates for of your landscaping empire will be the ones who can do it all, like a well oiled, lawn mowing, weed whacking, flower arranging machine.

Remember, your employees are the heart and soul of your business. Invest in their development, and they'll reward you with a level of dedication and expertise that will make your competitors green with envy (pun absolutely intended).

Encouraging a Positive and Productive Culture

Okay, let's talk about the secret ingredient that's going to take your landscaping business from good to great: company culture. Because let's face it, when it comes to the world of landscaping, things can get a little, well, dirty. But that doesn't mean your workplace has to be a drab, soul crushing environment where dreams go to die alongside the withered petunias.

Nope, you're going to nurture a culture that's as vibrant and thriving as the gardens you tend to. Start by embracing the quirkiness of your team – after all, who better to dream up outrageous lawn designs or master the art of floral origami than a bunch of self proclaimed plant nerds? Encourage them to bring their unique personalities to the job, and watch as your company transforms into a veritable oasis of creativity and camaraderie.

And don't be afraid to get a little weird – after all, what's a landscaping business without a touch of whimsy? Host quarterly team building events that involve things like synchronized mowing routines, lawnmower jousting, or a good old fashioned mulch flinging competition. Trust me, your employees will thank you for the opportunity to let their hair down (or, you know, their hard hats) and bond over a shared love of all things green and growing.

Remember, a happy team is a productive team. So pour that love and nurturing into your employees, and they'll return the favor by going above and beyond to ensure your landscaping business is the talk of the town – or, at the very least, the neighborhood gardening club.

Mastering the Art of Pricing

Calculating Accurate Cost Estimates

Pricing your landscaping services is no walk in the park, my friends. It's a delicate dance between covering your costs, staying competitive, and not leaving money on the table. But fear not, with a few strategic moves, you can master this art form and turn those green thumbs into greenbacks.

First and foremost, ditch the guesswork. Accurate cost estimates are the foundation of a bulletproof pricing strategy. Get your calculator out and start crunching the numbers – labor, materials, overhead, the whole nine yards. Break it down to the nitty gritty, because trust me, those small expenses can add up faster than a weed in a well tended garden.

Don't just rely on industry averages either. Every setting job is unique, with its own quirks and challenges. Factor in the size of the project, the intricacy of the design, and any special requirements your clients might have. And don't forget to account for the unexpected – because let's face it, Murphy's Law is alive and well in the landscaping world.

Once you've got a solid handle on your costs, it's time to add in a healthy profit margin. This is where the art comes in, my friends. You want to strike the perfect balance between being competitive and ensuring your business thrives. Experiment with different percentages, and don't be afraid to adjust as you go. After all, what works for one project might not fly for the next.

Determining Competitive Pricing Strategies

Now that you've got your costs covered, it's time to scope out the competition. Because let's be real, no one wants to be the landscaping equivalent of the guy selling hot dogs for $20 a pop.

Start by researching the pricing strategies of your local rivals. Are they offering flat rate packages or hourly rates? What about bundled services or à la carte options? Dig deep, my friends, and don't be afraid to get a little creative with your research methods. Heck, you might even want to consider going undercover as a potential client (just don't forget to wear your disguise).

But don't stop there. Look beyond your immediate competitors and keep an eye on industry trends. What are the big players in the game doing? Are there any new services or technologies popping up that could change the game? Stay on the cutting edge, and you'll be able to position your business as the industry innovator – with the pricing to match.

Remember, the key to a winning pricing strategy is finding that sweet spot between being affordable and being profitable. It's a delicate balance, but with a little elbow grease and a whole lot of creativity, you can make it happen. Who knows, you might even end up with a pricing model so ingenious, it becomes the envy of the landscaping world.

Offering Flexible Payment Options

Now, let's talk about the fun part – getting paid. Because let's be real, no matter how amazing your landscaping services are, if your clients can't pay the bill, it's all for naught.

That's why it's vital to offer a variety of payment options that cater to the diverse needs of your clientele. Think beyond the traditional cash or check, my friends. Embrace the digital age with credit card processing, mobile payment apps, and even the occasional cryptocurrency transaction (you never know when that eccentric millionaire with a fondness for Bitcoin might come knocking).

But don't stop there. Get creative with your payment plans, too. Offer flexible installment options, seasonal discounts, or even a loyalty program for your most dedicated green thumbed devotees. After all, the more ways you can make it easy for your clients to pay, the more likely they are to keep coming back (and bringing their friends).

And let's not forget about the importance of clear and transparent pricing. No one likes unpleasant surprises when it comes to their landscaping bill. Make sure your estimates are detailed, your invoices are straightforward, and your payment terms are easy to understand. Because the last thing you want is a disgruntled client who feels like they've been sold a bill of goods.

So there you have it, folks – the keys to mastering the art of pricing in the landscaping business. With a little elbow grease, a lot of creativity, and a healthy dose of business savvy, you'll be well on your way to turning those green thumbs into greenbacks in no time.

Streamlining Operations and Workflows

Developing Efficient Scheduling and Routing

In the fast paced world of landscaping, time is of the essence. Mastering the art of scheduling and routing can mean the difference between a well oiled machine and a chaotic mess. As the sun rises on your budding business, it's time to ditch the old school paper calendar and embrace the power of technology to take your operations to new heights.

First and foremost, invest in a powerful scheduling software that can seamlessly integrate with your team's mobile devices. We're talking about a platform that can effortlessly manage job assignments, improve routes, and provide real time updates to your clients. Imagine the satisfaction of watching your crew zip from one job site to the next, without a single hiccup or missed appointment.

But it's not just about the tech – it's about the strategy. Develop a comprehensive scheduling system that accounts for variables like weather, traffic patterns, and employee availability. Encourage your team to embrace this new way of working, as it not only boosts productivity but also helps them stay on top of their game. Plus, with instant access to schedules and job details, your clients will be blown away by your level of organization and responsiveness.

Remember, efficiency is the name of the game, and a well crafted scheduling and routing strategy can be the secret weapon that sets your landscaping business apart from the competition. So, embrace the digital age, simplify your operations, and watch as your business flourishes like a carefully tended garden.

Implementing Effective Inventory Management

As your landscaping business grows, so too will the demands on your inventory. Gone are the days of haphazardly grabbing supplies from the back of the truck – it's time to implement a system that keeps track of every leaf blower, lawnmower, and bag of fertilizer.

Start by creating a comprehensive inventory log, tracking not only the quantity of each item but also its condition, location, and usage history. This information will be essential when it comes to maintaining your equipment, reordering supplies, and ensuring that your team has access to the tools they need, when they need them.

But don't stop there – incorporate smart storage solutions to keep your inventory organized and accessible. Employ labeled shelves, bins, and racks to create a visual system that makes it easy for your team to quickly locate what they're looking for. And consider implementing a Just In-Time (JIT) inventory management approach, where you order supplies only as needed, minimizing waste and maximizing efficiency.

Remember, effective inventory management is about more than just keeping track of your assets – it's about enabling your team to work smarter, not harder. When your crew can quickly grab the right tool for the job, they'll be able to tackle projects with a level of speed and precision that'll leave your clients in awe. So, embrace the power of organization and watch as your landscaping business flourishes.

Utilizing Technology to Boost Productivity

In the ever evolving world of landscaping, utilizing the power of technology can be the secret to uncovering your business's true potential. From streamlining workflows to improving customer experiences, the right tech tools can transform your operation from a well oiled machine to a veritable juggernaut.

Start by investing in a suite of mobile apps and software solutions that can seamlessly integrate with your team's devices. Imagine the efficiency of having job details, client information, and even real time weather updates at your fingertips. This kind of connectivity can help your crew navigate the chaos of the day with the precision of a surgeon and the agility of a gazelle.

But technology isn't just about boosting productivity – it's also about delighting your clients. Embrace digital invoicing, online booking systems, and even augmented reality tools that allow your customers to visualize the final product before you even break ground. By incorporating these cutting edge solutions, you'll not only make efficient your operations but also demonstrate your commitment to providing an unparalleled level of service.

Of course, with great technology comes great responsibility. Ensure that your team is well versed in the latest tools and that your cybersecurity measures are as powerful as your lawnmower blades. After all, the last thing you want is for a data breach to derail your hard earned progress.

So, embrace the power of technology, let it turbocharge your productivity, and watch as your landscaping business reaches new heights of success. It's time to ditch the old school ways and usher in a new era of landscaping excellence.

Winning and Retaining Customers

Leveraging Networking and Referrals

In the cutthroat world of landscaping, it's not just about having a killer green thumb - it's about cultivating a thriving network that can help your business blossom. Forget the stuffy networking events filled with dull suits and forced small talk. If you really want to tap into the power of word of-mouth, you've got to get creative.

Start by embracing your inner social butterfly and casting a wide net. Attend community events, volunteer at the local garden center, or even host a backyard barbecue for your fellow landscaping enthusiasts. The key is to position yourself as the go to expert for all things green and growing, the kind of person people can't wait to tell their friends about.

And let's not forget the magic of referrals. Offer exclusive discounts or freebies to clients who send new business your way, and make sure to follow up with a heartfelt thank you. After all, nothing says "I appreciate you" quite like a handwritten note and a basket of freshly baked muffins (with a side of freshly mowed grass, of course).

Remember, the landscaping industry is built on relationships, not just raw talent. So get out there, shake some hands, and let your personality shine brighter than the sun kissed petals of a newly planted flower bed.

Delivering Exceptional Customer Service

In the world of landscaping, customer service isn't just a nicety - it's the lifeblood of your business. And we're not talking about the standard "smile and nod" routine. No, my friend, you need to take customer service to a whole new level, one that leaves your clients feeling like they've just discovered the secret garden of their dreams.

Start by anticipating your clients' needs before they even know they have them. Surprise them with timely updates, personalized recommendations, and a level of attention that makes them feel like the only person in your verdant universe. And when it comes to handling complaints or concerns, embrace your inner zen master and respond with a level of patience and understanding that would make even the Dalai Lama proud.

But it's not just about the big gestures - the little things can make all the difference, too. A handwritten thank you note, a personalized birthday card, or even a spontaneous bouquet of freshly harvested blooms can go a long way in building long lasting relationships with your customers.

Remember, in the world of landscaping, your clients aren't just hiring you to tame their overgrown gardens - they're investing in your expertise, your creativity, and your unwavering commitment to making their outdoor oasis a true reflection of their unique style and personality. So, roll up those sleeves, get your hands dirty, and show them what exceptional customer service really looks like.

Building Long Term Relationships

In the ever evolving world of landscaping, the true secret to success lies not in the latest gardening trends or the most cutting edge equipment, but in the power of long term relationships. After all, what's the point of having a meticulously manicured lawn if the client who commissioned it is long gone, replaced by a new face every season?

The key is to develop a genuine connection with your clients, one that goes deeper than the surface level transaction of simply mowing their grass or pruning their shrubs. Start by taking the time to really understand their unique needs, their personal style, and their long term vision for their outdoor oasis. Remember that every client is a snowflake, no two the same, and the more you can tailor your approach to their individual preferences, the more likely they'll be to stick with you for the long haul.

But it's not just about the initial courtship - maintaining those relationships requires a constant nurturing and care, like tending to a delicate bonsai tree. Stay in touch, check in regularly, and be proactive in offering new ideas and solutions that can help your clients' outdoor spaces evolve and thrive. And when life throws a curveball, be there to offer a steady hand and a sympathetic ear, reminding them that you're not just their landscaper, but a trusted partner in the ever changing setting of their lives.

Remember, in the world of landscaping, your clients aren't just paying for your expertise - they're investing in a long term relationship built on trust, respect, and a shared passion for creating the perfect outdoor oasis. So, roll up your sleeves, get to know them on a deeper level, and watch as your business blossoms into a verdant garden of loyal, lifelong customers.

Expanding Your Service Options

Exploring Complementary Landscaping Services

As a savvy landscaping entrepreneur, it's time to think beyond the traditional mow and-blow routine. Sure, keeping lawns pristine and hedges neatly trimmed is the bread and butter, but why settle for being just another lawncare drone when you can diversify and become a one stop-shop for all things green and growing?

Dip your toes into the lucrative world of full service landscaping, where you can offer everything from tree trimming and plant installation to outdoor lighting and water feature design. Become the landscaping equivalent of a Swiss Army knife - a trusted advisor who can transform a drab backyard into a veritable oasis of tranquility.

Believe it or not, many of your existing customers are craving a more comprehensive solution. They don't want to juggle multiple vendors for their landscaping needs; they want someone they can rely on to handle it all, from start to finish. By expanding your service options, you can position yourself as that indispensable partner, cementing your status as the go to landscaping authority in your community.

Diversifying Your Product and

Service Mix

Diversity is the spice of life, and the same principle applies to your landscaping business. Don't limit yourself to merely mowing lawns and trimming hedges - explore the vast, verdant world of ancillary services and products that can help your company blossom.

Think beyond the typical lawn care selections and venture into the realm of garden design, hardscaping, and outdoor living spaces. Offer custom built planter boxes, serene water features, or even whimsical outdoor art installations. Become a purveyor of high end patio furniture, grills, and other backyard accessories that can transform a dull plot of land into a veritable oasis.

And don't forget about the seasonal opportunities that can keep your cash flow flowing year round. Explore snow removal services during the winter months, or offer holiday lighting installations to add a touch of festive cheer to your clients' homes. By diversifying your product and service mix, you can position your business as a true one stop-shop, catering to the ever evolving needs of your perceiving customers.

Adapting to Changing Market Demands

In the fast paced world of landscaping, the only constant is change. Trends come and go, customer preferences shift, and the demands of the market can be as fickle as a freshly mowed lawn. To stay ahead of the curve, you'll need to keep a keen eye on the horizon, anticipating the next big thing before it hits the mainstream.

Stay abreast of the latest industry developments, from eco friendly landscaping techniques to the rise of smart home technology in outdoor spaces. Be the first to offer cutting edge services like robotic lawn mowing or solar powered irrigation systems. Embrace the power of data and analytics to understand your customers' evolving needs and tailor your services accordingly.

But don't just react to the market - be a trailblazer and shape it. Experiment with bold, unconventional ideas that push the boundaries of traditional landscaping. Who knows, your next big service offering might just be a custom designed treehouse or a living, breathing moss wall that turns heads and captivates imaginations. By staying responsive, novel, and attuned to the ever changing tides of the industry, you can ensure that your landscaping business remains a step ahead of the competition.

Navigating Regulatory Compliance

Understanding Local Zoning and Permit Laws

Starting a landscaping business is no walk in the park, especially when it comes to navigating the tangled web of local zoning and permit regulations. But fear not, my fellow green thumbed entrepreneurs – with a bit of strategic planning and a healthy dose of tenacity, you can transform these legal hoops into your personal jungle gym.

First things first, get to know your local government like the back of your calloused, dirt caked hands. Scour their websites, attend town hall meetings, and befriend the most cantankerous city planner you can find. Uncover the hidden secrets of your area's zoning laws, learning which neighborhoods are ripe for your verdant creations and which are better off left to the weeds.

Next, prepare to become the master of permits. From business licenses to landscaping specific approvals, you'll need to navigate a minefield of paperwork and red tape. Don't be daunted, though – approach each application with the same persistent enthusiasm you'd bring to taming an overgrown hedge. Charm the clerks, sweet talk the bureaucrats, and emerge victorious, permits in hand.

And remember, flexibility is key. Local regulations can change quicker than a weed's growth spurt, so stay responsive. Be ready to adapt your business plan, adapt your services, and even consider relocating to a more landscaping friendly jurisdiction if the need arises. After all, the true green thumb is the one that bends with the wind, not the one that snaps.

Complying with Environmental Regulations

In the world of landscaping, the only thing greener than your freshly manicured lawns should be your commitment to environmental compliance. Navigating the labyrinth of environmental regulations might seem daunting, but trust me, it's a dance you'll want to master if you plan on keeping your business out of hot water – and your clients out of the compost heap.

First, familiarize yourself with the latest eco friendly trends and effective techniques in the industry. From sustainable irrigation systems to organic pest control methods, staying ahead of the curve will not only keep you in the good graces of regulatory agencies, but also position you as a true green friendly pioneer in the eyes of your distinguishing clientele.

Next, dive deep into your local and state environmental regulations. Hazardous waste disposal, stormwater management, and chemical usage – these are just the tip of the iceberg when it comes to the compliance challenges you'll face. Invest in the training and resources necessary to ensure your team is well versed in these ever evolving rules and regulations.

And remember, it's not just about checking boxes – it's about embracing the spirit of environmental stewardship. Embody this commitment in your company culture, your marketing materials, and your day to-day operations. Your clients will appreciate your dedication, and you'll sleep soundly knowing that your thriving business is also nurturing the planet.

Ensuring Worker Safety and Liability Coverage

In the high stakes world of landscaping, safety should be your top priority – after all, you're dealing with everything from razor sharp lawnmowers to venomous critters lurking in the undergrowth. But fear not, my enterprising horticulturists – with the right strategies and precautions, you can transform your workplace into a verdant oasis of productivity and peace of mind.

First and foremost, familiarize yourself with the intricacies of worker's compensation laws and liability coverage. Dive headfirst into the murky depths of insurance policies, negotiating the most comprehensive protection for your team. Don't skimp on this – a single slip and-fall incident can leave you scrambling to pick up the pieces, both financially and emotionally.

Next, develop a comprehensive safety training program that puts your employees' well being at the forefront. From proper equipment handling to emergency response protocols, equip your team with the knowledge and tools they need to navigate the natural risks of the landscaping trade. Encourage a culture of accountability and vigilance, where every worker feels allowed to speak up and identify potential hazards.

And while you're at it, don't forget to safeguard your own liability. Invest in comprehensive general liability insurance to shield your business from the slings and arrows of disgruntled clients, wayward lawnmowers, and anything else the unpredictable world of landscaping might throw your way. Trust me, the peace of mind is worth every penny.

Mastering Effective Marketing Strategies

Developing a Comprehensive Marketing Plan

In the ever evolving terrain of the landscaping industry, a rock solid marketing plan is the cornerstone of your success. Forget about those one size-fits all templates - it's time to get real and create a strategy that's as unique as your business. Start by taking a in-depth look into your target audience. Who are these green thumbed individuals you're aiming to captivate? What makes them tick, and more importantly, what will make them choose you over the competition?

Once you've got a handle on your ideal client, it's time to get creative. Ditch the bland, generic marketing tactics and embrace your inner marketing maverick. Think outside the box, my friend. What if you organized a community garden cleanup day, complete with refreshments and a raffle for a free landscaping consultation? Or how about partnering with a local artist to create a series of whimsical yard art pieces that double as marketing materials? The options are endless, so get your brainstorming cap on and let your imagination run wild.

Remember, your marketing plan should be a living, breathing document that adapts and evolves alongside your business. Regularly review and refine your strategies, keeping a close eye on what's working and what needs a little TLC. Don't be afraid to experiment, take risks, and ultimately, have fun with the process. After all, when your marketing is as vibrant and dynamic as the sets you create, the clients will be lining up at your door.

Utilizing Traditional and Digital Advertising

In the fast paced world of landscaping, you need to be a marketing chameleon, seamlessly blending traditional and digital advertising tactics to reach your target audience. Start by embracing the power of good old fashioned print media. Think eye catching flyers, bold signage, and strategically placed advertisements in local publications. These classic methods may seem a bit old school, but they still hold the power to captivate and intrigue potential clients.

Now, let's talk digital. Dive headfirst into the world of search engine optimization (SEO), crafting a website that's a veritable oasis of information for your green fingered audience. Pepper your content with the right keywords and phrases, making it easy for your ideal clients to find you when they're searching for their next landscaping partner. And don't forget about the visual punch - stunning photography and video tours of your work can be the difference between a casual browser and a committed customer.

But the real magic happens when you harmonize your traditional and digital efforts. Employ the power of social media to intensify your message, sharing a tantalizing sneak peek of your latest project on Instagram, then driving traffic to your website with a strategically placed print ad. The key is to create a cohesive, cross platform marketing campaign that keeps your brand front and center, no matter where your potential clients are looking.

Leveraging Social Media and Online Platforms

In the digital age, social media is the ultimate playground for landscaping businesses looking to develop a loyal following. But forget about the cookie cutter approach - it's time to get downright quirky and unconventional. Think outside the perfectly curated feed and embrace the power of authentic, relatable content.

Start by showcasing the heart and soul of your business. Share behind the-scenes glimpses of your team in action, let your followers peek into your creative process, and don't be afraid to get a little goofy. After all, who says landscaping has to be all serious and staid? Inject a healthy dose of personality into your social media presence, and watch as your audience falls head over heels for your brand.

But it's not just about posting pretty pictures and witty captions. Channel the power of online platforms to engage with your community in meaningful ways. Host virtual Q&A sessions, offer exclusive discounts and promotions, or even crowdsource ideas for your next big project. By creating a sense of interactivity and connection, you'll not only build brand loyalty but also position yourself as a trusted authority in the landscaping realm.

Remember, social media is a dynamic, ever evolving setting, so stay nimble and adaptable. Regularly analyze your performance, experiment with new tactics, and be willing to change direction when something isn't resonating with your audience. With a healthy dose of creativity, a pinch of quirkiness, and a unwavering commitment to your brand, you'll be well on your way to social media stardom in no time.

Scaling Your Business for Growth

Identifying Opportunities for Expansion

So, you've laid the groundwork, built a solid foundation, and now you're ready to take your landscaping business to the next level. But where do you even begin? The key is to keep your finger on the pulse of your industry, constantly scanning the horizon for fresh opportunities to grow and expand.

Start by analyzing your current service products – are there any complementary services you could add to your menu? Maybe your clients are clamoring for tree trimming or garden design? Don't be afraid to think outside the box and experiment with new revenue streams. Just make sure they sync with your brand and expertise.

Next, take a detailed examination into your local market. Are there any underserved neighborhoods or communities that could benefit from your services? Perhaps there's an affluent suburb yearning for a high end, personalized landscaping experience. Or maybe a nearby industrial park is in desperate need of some green thumbed magic. The key is to identify pockets of demand and position your business as the go to solution.

And don't forget to keep an eye on emerging trends and technologies. Who knows, maybe self driving lawnmowers will be the next big thing, and you'll want to be the first landscaper in town to offer that cutting edge (pun intended) service.

The bottom line? Stay curious, stay adaptable, and always be on the lookout for that next big opportunity. After all, the landscaping industry is like a wild jungle – you've got to be nimble, inventive, and ready to pounce on the next big breakthrough.

Streamlining Processes and Automating Tasks

As your landscaping business grows, so too will the convolution of your operations. That's why it's critical to stay ahead of the curve by streamlining your processes and automating as many tasks as possible. Trust me, the last thing you want is to be drowning in a sea of spreadsheets and sticky notes, wondering where the heck you put that client's irrigation schedule.

Start by taking a long, hard look at your current workflows. Where are the bottlenecks? What tasks are eating up an inordinate amount of your team's time? Maybe it's scheduling appointments, or maybe it's tracking inventory – either way, identify those is a challenge and start exploring solutions.

Technology is your best friend here. Invest in strong scheduling software that can automatically improve routes and send out reminders to clients. Implement a cloud based inventory management system that can help you stay on top of supplies and equipment. Heck, you might even want to look into AI powered chatbots to handle customer inquiries and schedule consultations.

But don't forget the human element. Make sure your team is well trained and equipped to take advantage of these new tools and systems. Encourage a culture of continuous improvement, where everyone is encouraged to suggest ways to rationalize and automate. After all, your employees are the ones on the frontlines, and they just might have the best ideas for boosting efficiency.

Remember, time is money in the landscaping business. By streamlining your operations and automating repetitive tasks, you'll free up your team to focus on higher value work, deliver an even more exceptional customer experience, and ultimately, scale your business to new heights.

Securing Financing and Investing in Infrastructure

So, you've got big plans for your landscaping business – maybe you want to open a second location, invest in a fleet of state of-the art equipment, or even launch a fancy new e commerce platform. But the reality is, none of that can happen without the proper financing and infrastructure in place.

First things first, take a long, hard look at your financial situation. Do you have enough cash on hand to fund your expansion plans, or will you need to seek out additional financing? Explore options like small business loans, venture capital, or even crowdfunding platforms. Just be sure to do your homework, crunch the numbers, and choose a financing path that coordinates with your long term vision.

Once you've secured the necessary funds, it's time to start investing in the infrastructure to support your growth. That might mean upgrading your equipment, expanding your facilities, or even investing in a strong customer relationship management (CRM) system. Remember, every dollar you pour into your business should be laser focused on improving your operations, streamlining your workflows, and delivering an even more exceptional experience for your clients.

And don't forget about the power of partnerships. Reach out to other landscaping businesses, suppliers, or even complementary service providers and explore opportunities for mutually beneficial collaborations. Maybe you can share equipment, pool resources for bulk purchasing, or even co market your services to reach a wider audience.

The key is to approach this phase of your business with the same level of strategic thinking and attention to detail that you've applied to every other aspect of your operations. After all, your success isn't just about having a green thumb – it's about having the vision, the resources, and the savvy to turn that green thumb into a veritable gold mine.

Managing Finances and Cash Flow

Implementing Strong Accounting Practices

Ahh, the joys of number crunching and spreadsheet wizardry - the backbone of any thriving landscaping business. Listen up, my fellow green thumbed entrepreneurs, because proper accounting practices are the difference between sipping mojitos on a private island and drowning in a sea of unpaid invoices.

First things first, ditch the shoe box filled with crumpled receipts and embrace the power of cloud based accounting software. We're talking about platforms that can track every penny, from that big client contract to the spare parts you picked up on a whim. Think of it as your digital accountant, constantly keeping a watchful eye on your financial health.

But here's the real secret sauce: don't just input the numbers and call it a day. Nah, my friends, you need to become a financial ninja, analyzing those reports with the intensity of a professional poker player scrutinizing their hand. Look for patterns, spot potential issues, and make data driven decisions that will have your competitors green with envy.

And let's not forget about those pesky taxes. Stay on top of your obligations, whether it's quarterly estimated payments or end of-year filings. Trust me, the last thing you want is the IRS knocking on your door with their hand out, ready to take a bite out of your hard earned profits.

Monitoring Income, Expenses, and Profitability

Now, let's dive into the nitty gritty of cash flow management. This is where you separate the scene legends from the wannabes. Sure, raking in the dough is great, but it's all about knowing where that money is coming from and where it's going.

Start by tracking your income streams with the precision of a seasoned sniper. I'm talking meticulously categorized invoices, detailed job estimates, and a crystal clear understanding of your revenue sources. This will not only help you identify your most profitable services but also uncover hidden opportunities to diversify and expand.

But wait, there's more! Expenses, the bane of every business owner's existence, can make or break your green thumbed empire. Dig deep into those receipts and invoices, scrutinize every penny spent, and ruthlessly cut any wasteful spending. Trust me, those daily lattes and impulse equipment purchases can add up faster than a weed infested lawn.

And when it comes to profitability, don't just rely on gut instinct. Crunch the numbers, analyze your gross and net margins, and identify the services that are truly driving your bottom line. This intel will be indispensable as you strategize for growth, allocate resources, and make smart financial decisions that will have your accountant doing cartwheels.

Exploring Financing Options and Tax Incentives

Alright, let's talk about the elephant in the room: money. The lifeblood of any business, and often the thing that keeps landscaping entrepreneurs up at night, tossing and turning like a freshly mowed lawn.

But fear not, my friends! There are a plenty of financing options out there, waiting to be seized like a juicy weed out of a flowerbed. From traditional bank loans to alternative lenders, angel investors, and even crowdfunding platforms, the key is to explore every avenue and find the perfect fit for your unique financial needs.

And while you're at it, don't forget to take advantage of those oh so-sweet tax incentives. From deductions for fuel efficient equipment to credits for hiring military veterans, the tax code can be a veritable wealth of savings if you know where to look. Heck, you might even end up owing less than your neighbor's prized roses!

But remember, my green fingered friends, financing and taxes are not to be taken lightly. Consult with trusted financial advisors, comb through the fine print, and never, ever, try to pull a fast one on the IRS. Trust me, you don't want to be the landscaper who ended up in the slammer for creative accounting. Keep your nose clean, and those greenbacks will keep rolling in.

Ensuring Long Term Sustainability

Promoting Environmentally Friendly Practices

In a world increasingly conscious of its environmental impact, it's time to ditch the outdated notion that going green means sacrificing profits. In fact, embracing sustainable practices can not only benefit the planet, but also give your landscaping business a competitive edge. So, buckle up, because we're about to take a detailed examination into how you can transform your business into a eco friendly powerhouse.

First and foremost, let's talk about the big kahuna: your fleet of landscaping equipment. These gas guzzling beasts may have been the industry standard in the past, but it's time to evolve. Look into investing in electric or hybrid powered tools and vehicles - not only will they reduce your carbon footprint, but they'll also save you a pretty penny on fuel costs in the long run. And don't forget to properly maintain and service your equipment to maximize efficiency and minimize emissions.

Next, let's tackle the thorny issue of waste management. No more tossing those clippings and trimmings into the landfill - start composting on site and turn that green waste into nutrient rich soil for your clients' gardens. It's a win win scenario: you reduce your environmental impact while also providing a valuable resource for your customers.

Speaking of your customers, why not take it a step further and offer eco friendly landscaping services? Think drought resistant native plants, rain gardens, and low water irrigation systems. Not only will your clients appreciate the environmental benefits, but they'll also love the cost savings on their water bills. Plus, you'll stand out from the competition as the go to green thumb in town.

And let's not forget about your office operations. Implement a strong recycling program, switch to energy efficient lighting, and explore the use of renewable energy sources like solar panels. These small changes can add up quickly, resulting in a greener, more sustainable business that your employees and customers will be proud to be a part of.

Investing in Employee Development and Retention

In the landscaping business, your employees are the backbone of your operation. They're the ones who bring your client's visions to life, maintain the lush gardens and pristine lawns, and ensure that your business runs like a well oiled machine. So, it's time to start treating them like the valuable assets they are.

First and foremost, invest in comprehensive training programs that keep your team up to-date on the latest industry trends, techniques, and technologies. Encourage them to attend workshops, webinars, and industry events to continuously expand their knowledge and skill set. After all, the more knowledgeable and confident your employees are, the better equipped they'll be to deliver top notch service to your clients.

But it's not just about the technical know how - nurturing a positive and supportive work culture is just as essential. Implement regular team building activities, recognize and reward exceptional performance, and provide opportunities for career advancement. When your employees feel valued and invested in the company's success, they'll be more likely to stick around for the long haul.

And speaking of the long haul, don't forget to offer competitive compensation and benefits packages. In the current job market, top talent is in high demand, so you'll need to ensure that your landscaping business is seen as an employer of choice. Offer generous salaries, health insurance, retirement plans, and even perks like paid time off for volunteer work or further education.

By investing in your employees, you're not only building a loyal and skilled workforce, but you're also setting your business up for long term success. After all, happy, engaged employees are the key to delighted customers, and that's the foundation for a thriving, sustainable landscaping enterprise.

Continuously Innovating and Adapting to the Market

In the ever evolving world of landscaping, complacency is the kiss of death. If you want to ensure the long term viability of your business, you need to be constantly on the lookout for new trends, technologies, and opportunities that can give you a competitive edge.

Start by keeping a keen eye on the industry pulse. Attend trade shows, subscribe to landscaping publications, and network with other industry leaders to stay ahead of the curve. Pay attention to shifts in customer preferences, emerging eco friendly practices, and novel tools and equipment that could simplify your operations.

But don't just sit back and observe - be proactive in your approach to innovation. Encourage your team to brainstorm new ideas, experiment with cutting edge techniques, and explore ways to diversify your service selections. After all, the landscaping industry is ripe with untapped potential, and the businesses that are nimble and adaptable will be the ones that thrive in the long run.

Of course, innovation doesn't have to mean reinventing the wheel. Sometimes, it's about taking a tried and-true approach and putting a fresh spin on it. Maybe it's developing a proprietary software system to fine-tune your scheduling and routing, or creating a unique service package that caters to the specific needs of a particular market segment.

And let's not forget about the power of collaboration. Forge partnerships with complementary businesses, such as nurseries, irrigation specialists, or even eco friendly product manufacturers. By pooling your resources and expertise, you can create novel solutions that set your landscaping business apart from the competition.

Remember, the key to long term sustainability in the landscaping industry is a willingness to embrace change, take calculated risks, and constantly seek new ways to improve your products. So, get out there, stay curious, and never stop exploring the boundless possibilities that lie ahead.

Silas Meadowlark

www.ingramcontent.com/pod-product-compliance
Lightning Source LLC
Chambersburg PA
CBHW030507220526
45464CB00006B/2697